The Stuff Dreams Are Made Of.

Proudly supplying the equipment that helps the dreams of future champions come true. Since 1884.

Louisville Slugger®

Louisville Slugger®

NEW YORK YANKEES

DICK LALLY

BONANZA BOOKS

New York

First published in 1991 by Bonanza Books, distributed by Outlet Book
Company, Inc., a Random House Company, 225 Park Avenue South,
New York, New York 10003, by arrangement with MBKA.

ACKNOWLEDGMENTS

Majority of Player Photographs by Tom Dipace
Additional thanks to:
John Broggi — JKJ Sports Collectibles, Inc.
National Baseball Hall of Fame & Museum, Inc.

Printed and bound in the United States of America

Library of Congress Cataloging-in-Publication Data

Lally, Dick.
    The New York Yankees / by Dicky Lally.
        p.   cm. — (Louisville Slugger)
    Summary: An overview of the New York Yankees baseball team,
discussing its history, last season, great moments, records, and
prospects.
    ISBN 0-517-05788-3
    1. New York Yankees (Baseball team)—Juvenile literature.
[1. New York Yankees (Baseball team)] I. Title. II. Series.
GV875.N4L34   1991
796.357′64′097471—dc20   90-28328
                                                CIP
                                                AC

ISBN 0-517-05788-3

8 7 6 5 4 3 2 1

CONTENTS

"STUMP" MERRILL

MANAGER

This career minor league manager took over the Yankee reins from Bucky Dent on June 6, 1990. His stocky build (5 feet 8 inches, 190 pounds) inspired his nickname. As a player, Merrill was a good defensive catcher with a strong arm but a weak bat. With two home runs and a .234 batting average in six minor league seasons, Stump has proclaimed, "Me and the stick didn't get along." Blessed with an unquenchable enthusiasm, he has been compared to Tommy Lasorda as a positive clubhouse influence. Yankee left-hander Dave LaPoint has said, "Stump is always cheering, and you start cheering right along with him. You don't even know it." He has managed in the Yankee farm system since 1977. Though he didn't have an immediate impact on the Yankee won-lost record, he impressed nearly everyone as a strategist and team leader. Merrill is a gambler who will do anything to shake up the opposition. Under him the Yankees became more aggressive, bunting more often, utilizing the hit-and-run, and taking the extra base. Merrill turned Dave Righetti's season around by showing confidence in his ace reliever. His managerial philosophy is basic: "If two teams are evenly matched in talent, the club with the greater intensity will win." He led New York to a 37-45 record after the All-Star break, and it was a more competitive team than it had been in the first half. His multi-year contract was George Steinbrenner's last official act as head of the New York Yankees.

GREG CADARET
PITCHER

Though Cadaret has been with the Yankees for a year and a half, the team still doesn't seem quite sure of how to utilize him. Since joining the club as part of the Rickey Henderson deal, he has been a starter, a closer, a set-up man, and a left-handed specialist used to retire a single left-handed batter early or late in a game. In spring training, 1990, he was told he would share closing chores with Dave Righetti. That assignment lasted for all of 24 hours. This uncertainty has impeded the left-hander's progress. Cadaret did have some limited success as a starter in 1989. He pitched into the seventh inning in nine of his 13 starts, and his 4-5 record as a starter was largely the result of a lack of run support. He also pitched the two best games of his Yankee career as a starter. On August 7, 1989, he threw a two-hit complete-game shutout against the Cleveland Indians. A Brook Jacoby single in the eighth ended his no-hit bid. On September 2, 1989, he beat the California Angels, 2-1, in another complete game. His nine strikeouts in that contest were a major league career high. Despite this, history shows that Cadaret does his best work out of the bullpen. Left-handers have a hard time against him. As a left-handed set-up man for the Oakland A's, he went 5-2 with a 2.89 ERA in 1988. At the time of his trade to New York, he was repeating that success. The Yankees should find a way to return him to this role.

Age: 29			Bats: Left					Throws: Left		
	W	L	SV	G	CG	IP	HA	BB	SO	ERA
1990	5	4	3	54	0	121.1	120	64	80	4.15
Career	21	13	6	187	3	352.2	347	181	254	3.90

CHUCK CARY

PITCHER

Armed with a screwball he learned from former Yankee relief ace Luis Arroyo, Cary probably has the best stuff of any pitcher on the club, but he has been thwarted by a lack of runs and by his own intensity. Cary is an emotional pitcher who must learn to remain calm while on the mound. The home run was a particular nemesis for Cary in 1990. He allowed 21 homers, the highest total on the staff. In one game against the Brewers, on August 26, Cary surrendered only six hits in eight innings. However, three of those hits were home runs by Dave Parker, Rob Deer, and Mike Fielder. They forced Cary to leave the game with a no-decision. In a game against the Red Sox, Cary entered the fourth inning with a shutout. Three hits and two walks later, the game was tied 2-2, and the left-hander was headed for the showers. He later criticized Stump Merrill for the quick hook. Such performances were emblematic of Cary's season. However, when Cary was good, he was very good. He finished second on the club in strikeouts (134) despite pitching only 156⅔ innings. He walked only 55 batters, though he did throw 11 wild pitches. His 4.19 ERA was greatly inflated by a few horrendous outings. With better offensive support, he could have posted a winning record. It would also help if he could manage to avoid crashing into teammates. A collision with the rather large Steve Balboni left Cary with a concussion that forced him out of a game against the Tigers.

Age: 31			Bats: Left					Throws: Left		
	W	L	SV	G	CG	IP	HA	BB	SO	ERA
1990	6	12	0	28	2	156.2	155	55	134	4.19
Career	12	20	3	108	4	336.1	307	115	278	3.83

LEE GUETTERMAN

PITCHER

Guetterman came to the Yankees from Seattle after the 1987 season. As a starter-reliever with the Mariners, he had just posted an impressive 11-4 record with a losing club. Druing his first season in New York, his versatility left him with such an ill-defined role it limited his effectiveness. At the start of spring training in 1989, there was even some doubt he would remain on the Yankee roster. The Yankees had acquired pitchers Dave LaPoint and Andy Hawkins as free agents and Jimmy Jones and Lance McCullers in a trade. Luckily for the Yankees, Guetterman did win a job. Used primarily as a long reliever, after McCullers failed in that role, he emerged as the Yankees' most dependable pitcher. Guetterman started that year with 30⅔ scoreless innings, a major league record for a reliever at the start of the season. He was unscored upon until his 20th appearance, when he surrendered five runs in two innings against California. As an occasional closer whenever Dave Righetti was either unavailable or ineffective, he was able to notch a career-high 13 saves. Guetterman carried this success into the 1990 season, though he didn't get many opportunities to close. A revivified Righetti limited Guetterman to only two saves. However, his 11 wins made him the first pitcher to lead the Yankees in victories without starting a single game. Guetterman's 3.39 ERA was the best among Yankees with 90 or more innings pitched.

Age: 32				Bats: Left				Throws: Left	
	W	L	SV	G	CG	IP	HA	BB	SO	ERA
1990	11	7	2	64	0	93	80	26	48	3.39
Career	28	21	15	223	3	430.1	461	133	196	4.10

ANDY HAWKINS

PITCHER

Before the start of 1990 there were actually rumors that the Pirates were going to send Barry Bonds to the Yankees for Andy Hawkins. Mr. Bonds went on to have an MVP year with Pittsburgh, as he helped lead his team to the NL East flag. So what kind of year did Mr. Hawkins have? This kind: he was involved in two no-hitters against the Chicago White Sox, one of which he threw—and he lost both of them. His win against the Detroit Tigers on September 30, 1989, proved to be his last victory at Yankee Stadium until August 6, 1990, when he defeated Cleveland, 3-1. He made three starts against the AL East champion Boston Red Sox and failed to last more than a third of an inning in any of them. His 1990 totals against Boston read like the French casualty list from Agincourt: 3 games—1 inning pitched—18 earned runs, 162.00 ERA. By the season's final month, he had been yanked from the starting rotation so that the Yankee brass could evaluate its younger pitchers. Yet he did have games, particularly after the arrival of Stump Merrill, in which he performed brilliantly. Unfortunately, when he pitched his best, his team didn't score. Hawkins threw 11 shutout innings against the Twins without winning the game. It was that kind of season. Through it all Hawkins never lost his professional demeanor. If you trust his history, he's a good bet to bounce back in 1991. His arm is sound, and he's been a big winner in the past.

Age: 31			Bats: Right					Throws: Right		
	W	L	SV	G	CG	IP	HA	BB	SO	ERA
1990	5	12	0	28	2	157.2	156	82	74	5.37
Career	80	85	0	261	26	1468.2	1483	570	74	4.14

DAVE LAPOINT
PITCHER

He's been around for so long it's almost hard to believe that this left-hander won't turn 32 until the middle of the 1991 season. LaPoint started his pro career with the Milwaukee Brewers. He was traded with outfielders Sixto Lezcano and David Green and pitcher Lary Sorensen to St. Louis on December 12, 1980, for pitchers Pete Vuckovich and Rollie Fingers and catcher Ted Simmons. That deal helped win a pennant for both clubs. LaPoint was 9-3 for the 1982 world champion Cardinals. Since then he has pitched for San Francisco, Detroit, San Diego, the Chicago White Sox, Pittsburgh, and the Yankees. He even served a brief second tour with St. Louis. In 1988 he won a career-high 14 games, and he signed with New York as a free agent on December 3 of that year. But 1989 was not a rewarding season. Though he had a five-game winning streak early in the season, he was less than impressive in most of those outings. LaPoint won only one more game, as a small tear in the left rotator cuff kept him on the disabled list for most of the summer. The injury required arthroscopic surgery. It was predicted he might rejoin the club in mid-1990. But LaPoint surprised the team's doctors by making a strong comeback and was with the Yankees on Opening Day. He was third on the team in wins, and only Tim Leary had more starts and innings pitched. With the Yankees desirous of evaluating their younger pitchers, LaPoint was yanked from the rotation in September.

Age: 31				Bats: Left					Throws: Left	
	W	L	SV	G	CG	IP	HA	BB	SO	ERA
1990	7	10	0	28	2	157.2	180	57	67	4.11
Career	80	85	1	292	11	1482	1588	553	799	3.98

TIM LEARY

PITCHER

In 1990 Leary was the only Yankee with more than 200 innings pitched, and he led the club in strikeouts and starts. His 4.11 ERA was inflated by a few horrendous outings. Had he received better support, he would have been a 15-game winner rather than a 19-game loser. Leary, whose split-fingered fastball breaks in an eccentric manner, did throw 23 wild pitches. No other major leaguer was charged with as many as 16. His best outing of the year may have come on July 9 against Seattle. He pitched 8⅔ innings of two-hit ball and combined with Lee Guetterman for a 1-0 win. His 18th loss of the season on September 9 was historic: it allowed the Oakland A's to complete a season's sweep (12-0) of the Yankees. Shortly after the defeat, Leary was yanked from the starting rotation. Management wanted to spare him the stigma of becoming the major leagues' first 20-game loser since Oakland's Brian Kingman in 1980. Last year represented Leary's second tour with a New York team. He started his pro career with the New York Mets, who touted him as "the next Tom Seaver." An elbow injury suffered on a rainy day in his first major league start postponed any early success. It wasn't until 1988 that he fulfilled some of those expectations as a Dodger. He won 17 games and helped lead his club to a world championship. He was traded to Cincinnati during the 1989 season. On December 12, 1989, the Yankees acquired him and Van Snider for Hal Morris and Rodney Imes.

Age: 33			Bats: Right						Throws: Right	
	W	L	SV	G	CG	IP	HA	BB	SO	ERA
1990	9	19	0	31	6	208	202	78	138	4.11
Career	54	75	1	199	21	1039.1	1061	322	682	3.79

PASCUAL PEREZ

PITCHER

With his eccentric behavior, flamboyant pitching style, and uncontrollable outspokenness, he is the Yankees' Wizard of Odd. After coming over from Montreal as a free agent, Perez started the season as if he was going to more than justify New York's $5 million investment in him. Despite winning only one of his first three stints, he pitched impressively and seemed bound for a big season if the team would only score some runs for him. Then a sore shoulder put him on the disabled list. Weeks of rest and therapy brought little relief. Doctors finally discovered a partially torn rotator cuff. Perez underwent surgery, and a full recovery was predicted. That would be splendid news for the Yankee pitching staff. If healthy, Perez could be the club's ace. He won 29 games in two seasons with the Atlanta Braves (1983-84), and his 7-0 record helped turn the 1987 Montreal Expos into unexpected contenders. His ERA with Montreal over three seasons was a glittering 2.88. He struck out 341 in 456⅔ innings while walking only 105. That strikeout-to-walk ratio was among the best in the majors. Perez started the 1989 season in a drug rehabilitation center. Pronounced clean, he opened the season without benefit of a full spring training and lost his first seven decisions. However, he managed to right himself. On a staff boasting Bryn Smith, Dennis Martinez, and Mark Langston, Perez was the club's most effective starter in the final months of the pennant race.

Age: 34			Bats: Right					Throws: Right		
	W	L	SV	G	CG	IP	HA	BB	SO	ERA
1990	1	2	0	3	0	14	8	3	12	1.29
Career	65	64	0	193	21	1170.1	1099	320	781	3.45

ERIC PLUNK

PITCHER

The hard-throwing reliever had an almost unnoticed good year. In 1989 the Yankees tried him in a variety of spots, including starter and occasional closer. The multiplicity of roles was not a benefit. He has yet to show the stamina required of a starter. He loses his best stuff after the early innings, and he doesn't yet have enough pitches to compensate. Last season he inherited the right-handed set-up role after Lance McCullers (with Clay Parker) was sent to Detroit for Matt Nokes. Plunk thrived in this position. His 2.72 ERA was his major league career low, and his 6-3 record gave him the best winning percentage on the team. His September 22 victory over Boston ended a seven-game Yankee losing streak. Plunk also had his team's best strikeout-to-innings pitched ratio, though his control is still not what it should be. His worst outings were marred by numerous walks. At 26 he was already the answer to a trivia question. The right-hander is the only player to be traded for Rickey Henderson twice. Plunk started his pro career after being picked by New York in the 1981 June draft. He played in the organization for four years without spending any time on the major league roster. On December 8, 1984, he was traded with pitchers Jose Rijo, Jay Howell, Tim Birtsas, and outfielder Stan Javier to the Oakland A's for Henderson. On June 21, 1989, he returned to the Yankees (with pitcher Greg Cadaret and outfielder Luis Polonia) in the deal that sent Rickey back to the A's.

Age: 27			Bats: Right					Throws: Right		
	W	L	SV	G	CG	IP	HA	BB	SO	ERA
1990	6	3	0	47	0	72.2	58	43	67	2.72
Career	29	24	8	204	0	470.1	384	310	419	3.96

JIM WALEWANDER

INFIELD

Walewander was signed to a triple-A contract by the Yankees on December 10, 1990. He will start spring training in minor league camp. The release of Wayne Tolleson could provide the opening for an eventual big league job for the infielder. Walewander was originally signed by the Detroit Tigers in 1983. On December 27, 1989, the Yankees drafted him as a six-year minor league free agent. While working his way up the Tigers' minor league ladder, Walewander was named to four straight All Star teams (1983–86). He made his major league debut with Detroit on May 31, 1987. He got his first major league hit in that game, a double off Minnesota's Bert Blyleven. His only major league home run came against California's Willie Fraser on September 26, 1987. Walewander's greatest assets are his versatility and his speed. Combined, they make him a perfect utility man. Though primarily a second baseman, he plays third base and shortstop with equal proficiency. Like the departed Tolleson, Walewander is a switch-hitter and a skilled bunter. In 1988 he tied for the Tiger lead in sacrifice hits (10), despite having accumulated only 175 at-bats. Walewander is also an excellent base-stealer. He led the Appalachian League (A) in stolen bases during his first year of pro ball. That started a string of four consecutive seasons with 25 or more base thefts. As a Tiger in 1988 he stole 11 bases in 15 attempts, in spite of starting in only 59 games.

Age: 28			Bats: Both						Throws: Right			
	G	AB	H	2B	3B	HR	R	RBI	BB	SO	SB	BA
1990	9	5	1	1	0	0	1	1	0	0	1	.200
Career	150	234	51	9	1	1	48	11	19	32	33	.217

MIKE WITT

PITCHER

The California Angels sent Witt to the Yankees during the 1989 season as payment for right fielder Dave Winfield. Three years earlier, both players would have been considered untouchables. In 1987 Witt was a 16-game winner and possessor of one of the best curveballs in the major leagues. Former teammate Reggie Jackson had dubbed it the "Mercedes Bends." It helped Witt rack up 100 wins and a perfect game before his 29th birthday. In 1986 his 18 victories led the AL West champion Angels. He faced Roger Clemens in the opening game of that season's American League playoffs and came away with a five-hit, 8-1 victory. This promising career began to unravel in 1988, when Witt suffered his first losing season (13-16) in the majors. It got even worse in 1989, as Witt posted a career low in wins (nine) and a career high in ERA (4.54). His strikeouts-to-innings pitched ratio was in steady decline. It was hypothesized throughout the league that Witt had become so enamored of his curveball that he had neglected his potent fastball. With disuse came a loss of velocity. Witt dusted off his heater in 1990, and the results were encouraging. Mixing fastballs with his still deadly curve, he was once again effective in a season curtailed by injury. Witt's record was deceptive. He was victimized by a usually reliable Yankee defense. His 0.78 unearned run average was the eighth highest in the American League and a whopping 35 points above the circuit's average.

Age: 30			Bats: Right							Throws: Right
	W	L	SV	G	CG	IP	HA	BB	SO	ERA
1990	5	6	0	16	2	96.2	106	34	60	4.47
Career	114	113	6	330	72	2062	2019	690	1343	3.79

SCOTT SANDERSON

PITCHER

A belated Christmas gift for the Yankees. The right-hander became a free agent after winning 17 games for Oakland in 1990. According to baseball rules, a club is not entitled to compensation if it loses a free agent unless it has offered arbitration to that player. Oakland dangled arbitration before Sanderson with the expectation that he would reject it. In fact, the A's had already signed the less pricey Eric Show to replace him. Sanderson shocked the A's by accepting their offer. Already saddled with baseball's highest payroll, Oakland was reluctant to have yet another millionaire ballplayer on its roster, so they sold him to the Yankees. On December 29 Sanderson and New York reached agreement on a two-year $4 million dollar contract. Sanderson comes to his new club armed with a first-rate curveball and pinpoint control. He has been an effective pitcher when healthy, and he has been particularly fit since undergoing back surgery in 1988. His 17 wins in 1990 were a career high. His previous best had been a 16-victory season for Montreal in 1980. Most important, Sanderson's 28 wins over the last two years are more than any other Yankee starter can claim. He also has the intangible asset of having played with a winner. An added bonus: Immediately after signing with the Yankees, Sanderson helped persuade friend and fellow free agent Mike Witt to rejoin the club. Witt, Sanderson, and Tim Leary should give New York a solid Big Three at the top of its pitching staff.

Age: 34			Bats: Right						Throws: Right	
	W	L	S	G	CG	IP	HA	BB	SO	ERA
1990	17	11	0	34	2	206.1	205	66	128	3.88
Career	115	100	5	343	34	1826.1	1772	478	1209	3.59

BOB GEREN
CATCHER

His 1990 batting average did not measure up to the fine .288 he posted in 1989, when he was named to the Topps Rookie All-Star Team. Geren did, however, hit eight home runs in only 277 at-bats. Not exactly Kevin Maas territory, but when combined with his 1989 totals (9 in 205 at-bats) it does indicate that he could do some damage at the plate if he were handed the full-time catcher's job. No doubt Yankee pitchers would be pleased by that move. Despite Rick Cerone's lively bat in 1990 and Matt Nokes's left-handed power, Geren is the man Yankee hurlers want behind the plate. He is a fluid receiver with a strong arm, and he calls an excellent game. Geren honed his defensive skills while spending parts of 11 seasons in the minor leagues. Originally signed by the Padres in June 1979, he was the player to be named later in the famous 10-player trade in 1980 that sent reliever Rollie Fingers to the St. Louis Cardinals. Geren joined the Yankee organization in 1986. He played 10 games with the major league club in 1988 and was promoted to the Yankee roster again on May 16, 1989. In his first three games after that call-up he went 5-for-12 with two home runs. His .454 slugging average that year was the third highest on the club for those appearing in at least 50 games. Geren does drive in runs and is fearless in the clutch. He strikes out too often, but his power and defense make him a valuable player for the Yankees.

Age: 29				Bats: Right						Throws: Right		
	G	AB	H	2B	3B	HR	R	RBI	BB	SO	SB	BA
1990	110	277	59	7	0	8	21	31	13	73	0	.213
Career	185	492	119	12	1	17	47	58	27	120	0	.242

MATT NOKES

CATCHER

The Yankees were after Nokes for the better part of two years. During the 1990 season they finally landed him in a deal that sent pitchers Clay Parker and Lance McCullers to the Tigers. Nokes joined the Tigers late in 1986 and in 1987 won attention with his 32 home runs. That was the 12th highest home-run total by a rookie in baseball history. Injuries and a lack of playing time have kept him substantially below that mark since then. He is a legitimate power hitter with a left-handed stroke that is perfect for Yankee Stadium. However, if he is to exceed his 1990 slugging totals, he is going to have to get more playing time, and that could be a problem. Nokes might be a man without a position. Though he joined the Tigers as a catcher, his skills behind the plate are still too limited to warrant giving him the everyday job. First base might be an option on another team, but with Mattingly, Maas, and Balboni on the roster, Nokes has little chance of seeing any playing time there. Left field could indirectly supply an opportunity. Depending on the status of Hensley Meulens, Mel Hall, and Oscar Azocar, Kevin Maas could end up in the outfield. That would open up the designated hitter spot for Nokes. A Nokes-Balboni platoon at that position would be ideal. Nokes could also compete for the left-field job and let Maas handle the DH chores. If he is going to stay on the team, the Yankees have to find a spot for him.

Age: 27			Bats: Left						Throws: Right			
	G	AB	H	2B	3B	HR	R	RBI	BB	SO	SB	BA
1990	136	351	87	9	1	11	33	40	24	47	2	.248
Career	506	1539	402	54	3	71	175	226	112	222	5	.261

STEVE BALBONI
FIRST BASE

When Reggie Jackson first saw the massive Steve Balboni, he said, "It looked as though the pitcher was throwing to a condominium!" During a game against Detroit last season, Chuck Cary collided with Balboni on a fielding play. The Yankee pitcher was led from the field with a concussion. The first baseman stayed in the game and hit a home run. Balboni originally signed with the Yankees in 1978 and built a reputation as a minor league slugger. Because the Yankee roster was overladen with superstars, he spent only parts of three seasons (1981-83) on the big league club and did not win a regular spot. A trade to the Kansas City Royals after the 1983 season gave him the chance to play every day, and he became one of the league's top home-run hitters. His 36 home runs led the 1985 world champion Royals. After a brief stint in Seattle, Balboni rejoined the Yankees in 1989. He was platooned at DH and occasionally spelled Don Mattingly at first. The result was 17 home runs and 59 RBIs in only 300 at-bats. Last year, though he batted only .196, he again hit 17 home runs in only 266 at-bats. Considering how Yankee Stadium inhibits right-handed sluggers, the power totals are commendable, and Balboni would undoubtedly raise his average with more regular use. He is not a one-dimensioinal player. During Mattingly's absence, Balboni showed a facile glove at first base. He doesn't run much, though. His last stolen base came in 1985. It's the only one of his career.

Age: 34				Bats: Right						Throws: Right		
	G	AB	H	2B	3B	HR	R	RBI	BB	SO	SB	BA
1990	116	266	51	6	0	17	24	34	35	91	0	.192
Career	958	3115	711	127	11	181	351	495	273	854	1	.228

ALVARO ESPINOZA

SHORTSTOP

Defensively, Espinoza is the best Yankee shortstop since Phil Rizzuto. He turns the double-play as well as any shortstop in baseball. He has excellent range and a strong throwing arm. After hitting a surprising .282 in 1989, he suffered through a season-long slump in 1990. Espinoza noted, "I haven't hit the ball so well, so I have to play good defense. If I don't, I'm out of here." It may take more than just a golden glove to keep him in the lineup during the upcoming season. His offensive numbers were the worst of any regular shortstop in the American League, as he starred in the Bronx version of "The Invisible Man." His .224 batting average was not enhanced by a puny 16 extra-base hits. An impatient hitter, his 16 walks contributed to a miniscule .258 on-base percentage. Espinoza is quick, but he is not particularly fast, and he has shown no signs of being a potent base-stealer. He is a fine bunter, one of the best in baseball, but that singular skill will not guarantee him a spot in the Yankee batting order. The emergence of Yankee minor league shortstop Carlos Rodriguez could threaten Espinoza's daily presence in the lineup. Rodriguez is a pesky hitter who has shown an ability to get on base. To answer his challenge, Espinoza must either return to his 1989 hitting level or learn how to draw a base on balls more frequently. The return of hitting coach Frank Howard—an Espinoza favorite—might revive the shortstop's bat in 1991.

Age: 29		Bats: Right								Throws: Right	
	G	AB	H	2B	3B	HR	R	RBI	BB	SO	SB	BA
1990	150	438	98	12	2	2	31	20	16	54	1	.224
Career	369	1043	264	38	3	2	91	71	32	133	4	.253

DON MATTINGLY
FIRST BASE

The Yankees' primary marquee player missed a large portion of the 1990 season because of a protruding disc. But even before his stint on the disabled list, it was apparent that Mattingly wasn't himself. If you were to use batting average as the sole barometer, he got off to the best start of his career. However, even when he was flirting with .400 during the first month of the season, the Mattingly power was noticeably absent. His hits were more of the ground-ball variety rather than the screaming line drives fans have come to expect. Mattingly went on the DL on July 24 and did not return to the lineup until September 21. In that game, a 3-0 loss to Boston, he went 1-for-4. One week later he had his first two-RBI game of the season. On September 30 he went 2-for-3 against the Milwaukee Brewers and drove in three runs. That performance convinced him that he was back to full health. In the clubhouse that evening he said, "As far as coming back, I think I've accomplished what I wanted to do. I know I'll be fine for next year. I just have to keep up the work." The return of a healthy Mattingly is a must if the Yankees are to have any hope of a resurgence. The 1985 MVP is still the best first baseman in the league and, at his best, he is one of the game's most lethal clutch hitters. He usually does his best hitting with men in scoring position. Mattingly already has more 100-RBI seasons (five) than Yankee demigod Mickey Mantle.

Age: 29			Bats: Left								Throws: Left	
	G	AB	H	2B	3B	HR	R	RBI	BB	SO	SB	BA
1990	102	394	10	16	0	5	40	42	28	20	1	.256
Career	1117	4416	1310	288	15	169	655	759	342	258	9	..297

STEVE SAX
SECOND BASE

In 1990, Sax experienced his worst offensive season since 1984. In late August he was dropped to the ninth spot in the batting order. It was the first time he had batted ninth, though he had batted eighth in several games with the Dodgers (who do not, of course, operate with a designated hitter). Sax responded to the demotion by going 3-for-8 in the two games and driving in the winning run in the 11th inning of a 4-3 victory over Milwaukee. After that game he returned to the more familiar number two spot in the lineup and hit well for the remainder of the season. His .260 batting average was 27 points lower than the career mark he toted into the 1990 season. It was also 55 points lower than his .315 of 1989. That he finished second to Roberto Kelly in the team batting race underscores the hitting malaise that gripped the Yankees throughout the season. But Sax's season was not filled with gloom. He finished second to Rickey Henderson in the stolen-base race (43), and his 42 RBIs placed him third on the team. It was his third straight season of 40 or more steals. Sax's defense was exemplary. Despite his batting woes, he never lost the competitive fire that has been his trademark since he broke into the major leagues in 1981. His on-field intensity doesn't suppress his natural wit in the clubhouse. He is famed throughout the league for his devastating send-up of comedian Andrew Dice Clay.

Age: 31			Bats: Right							Throws: Right		
	G	AB	H	2B	3B	HR	R	RBI	BB	SO	SB	BA
1990	155	615	160	24	2	4	70	42	49	46	43	.260
Career	1404	5578	1583	209	40	39	732	438	464	496	376	.284

STEVE FARR
PITCHER

Just when the Yankees seemed committed to a new era of fiscal responsibility, they opened their coffers and handed Steve Farr a three-year $6.3 million contract. Was this a risky move? Perhaps. But it was also a necessary one. Farr has been in the major leagues since 1984. He started his major league career with the Cleveland Indians and was traded to Kansas City in 1985. During his first three years with the Royals he was the set-up man for Dan Quisenberry and he performed ably. In 1988 and 1989 he was used as a closer, with mixed results. He saved 20 games and had a 2.50 ERA in 1988, but his ERA soared to 4.12 the following season. In 1990 he was named Kansas City's "Pitcher of the Year." Used chiefly in long relief, he set a career high in wins (13) and had a 1.98 ERA. In six starts he was 5-1 with a 1.47 ERA. It is always a gamble to sign a veteran player who just posted his best numbers in his final year before free agency. Farr has also been a much better pitcher on artificial turf than on the grass that covers the Yankee Stadium diamond. However, it is now obvious that he was signed as insurance against the possible loss of Dave Righetti. With Rags now in San Francisco, Farr will have to share the stopper's role with Lee Guettermann. Will he be up to the job? Replacing the Yankees' all-time save leader will be difficult, but Farr is known as a tenacious performer. If this gamble pays off, his expensive contract will have been a bargain.

Age: 34			Bats: Right						Throws: Right	
	W	L	SV	G	CG	IP	HA	BB	SO	ERA
1990	13	7	1	57	1	127.0	99	48	94	1.98
Career	37	35	50	320	1	627.0	575	249	513	3.33

JESSE BARFIELD

RIGHT FIELD

New York traded top prospect Al Leiter to the Toronto Blue Jays for Barfield on April 30, 1989. Barfield was supposed to supply power in the middle of the order, and he has done that. In 1990 he was second in team home runs to Don Mattingly and his 25 home runs led the Yankees in 1990. His 78 RBIs were also a team high, an especially laudable figure considering the team's paucity of base runners. Like many sluggers, Barfield is a big swinger who tends to strike out often. His 150 Ks in 1990 tied a career high and set a Yankee single-season record. He has learned to offset the strikeouts by walking. He has led the Yankees in bases on balls in each of the last two seasons. Barfield has shown impressive power since his first full year in the majors. In 1983 he hit 27 home runs in only 388 at-bats. In 1986, while still with Toronto, he led the American League in home runs (40) and reached career bests in runs (107), hits (170), and RBIs (108). A fast runner, Barfield has stolen as many as 22 bases in a season (1985), but he has failed to reach double figures since then. He simply doesn't run that often. Besides his power, Barfield is best known for his throwing arm. It is the best right-field gun in the league. He usually leads the AL in assists, despite the fact that runners rarely challenge him. Barfield has a reputation as a consummate team player whose work ethic is an inspiration to his peers.

Age: 31				Bats: Right						Throws: Right		
	G	AB	H	2B	3B	HR	R	RBI	BB	SO	SB	BA
1990	153	476	117	21	2	25	69	78	82	150	4	.246
Career	1314	4380	1142	202	30	222	670	661	506	1127	64	.261

MEL HALL
OUTFIELD

Hall made a lot of headlines in New York during the 1990 season. Unfortunately, too many of them were for incidents that occurred off the field. He had numerous altercations with Yankee management. Stump Merrill benched him on two occasions for failing to hustle. Yankee brass considered him a bad influence on since-departed rookie Deion Sanders (though whether *anyone* is able to influence Neon Deion is a matter of some debate), and he got into a heated confrontation with at least one New York reporter while maintaining frosty relations with several others. Immediately after the season ended, he was picked up and charged with the illegal possession of an endangered species. It seems he kept two cheetahs as house pets! Animal rights activists were calling for his head. This behavior, when coupled with the emergence of lefty slugger Kevin Maas, will probably make Hall an expendable Yankee. New York tried to deal him to Oakland late last season and continued to peddle him when the season ended. That's too bad, because New York could use his left-handed power in the lineup. Hall is in the Oscar Gamble mold: a player with an ideal Yankee Stadium swing. During his first year with the club (1989), he hit 17 home runs in only 361 at-bats. Last year his .433 slugging percentage was the third highest on the club. Mel has always had the talent, but he's in danger of running himself out of baseball.

Age: 30			Bats: Left						Throws: Left			
	G	AB	H	2B	3B	HR	R	RBI	BB	SO	SB	BA
1990	113	360	93	23	2	12	41	46	6	46	0	.258
Career	958	3137	865	170	20	100	431	454	211	478	27	.276

ROBERTO KELLY

CENTER FIELD

Kelly was the Yankees' best player in 1990. After hitting a solid .302 with 35 steals in 1989, he continued to improve at the plate in 1990. A slow start kept his average at a lower but still respectable .285. However, he set major league career highs in doubles (32), triples (4), home runs (15), RBIs (61), runs (85), stolen bases (42), and slugging (.418). His home-run total was especially surprising. Kelly had never hit more than 13 in any season, majors or minors, and Yankee Stadium is not generous to right-handed hitters. The center fielder was especially productive after the All-Star break. During one stretch in August (19-26), he hit .484 with two home runs, 5 RBIs, and 7 runs scored. His defense was eye-catching, though he is still prone to the occasional mental gaffe and has been known to miss the cutoff man. Experience should minimize those mistakes. Physically, he is gifted with Gold Glove tools. During his first season with New York, a perhaps overprotective Dallas Green usually batted him eighth in the Yankee lineup despite Kelly's roadrunner speed and productive bat. Last year, Kelly hit in every lineup spot except fourth. Where he batted didn't seem to make any difference to him. In the season's final months he settled into the leadoff spot and thrived. He can be expected to stay at the top of the lineup, but he must cut down on his strikeouts (148) and increase his walks.

Age: 26			Bats: Right							Throws: Right		
	G	AB	H	2B	3B	HR	R	RBI	BB	SO	SB	BA
1990	162	641	183	32	4	15	85	61	33	148	42	.285
Career	360	1211	349	57	8	26	171	123	82	267	91	.288

JIM LEYRITZ
THIRD BASE/CATCHER/OUTFIELD

Jim Leyritz's most memorable home run to date may have been one he didn't hit. On September 9, 1990, he hit an obvious home run off California's Mark Langston. Unfortunately, third base umpire Tim Welke ruled it foul. A later replay proved that the ball was indeed fair, but that didn't placate Leyritz, who was tossed from the game after throwing his bat and helmet. Leyritz was a non-roster player who was brought up to the Yankees as part of their mid-season youth movement. His versatility made him a valuable acquisition. He played most of the season at third base but spent some time in left field and made an impression on the Yankee management when he went behind the plate late in the season. His receiving skills shouldn't have come as a surprise; he spent most of his minor league career as a catcher. At Albany in 1989 he played 67 games at that position while leading the Eastern League (double-A) in hitting (.315) and on-base percentage (.423). That performance earned him a spot on the Eastern League All-Star team. It also caught the attention of the Yankee brass, who moved Leyritz up to triple-A in 1990 prior to his promotion to New York. Leyritz has been a good line-drive hitter thoughout his minor-league career. His 10 home runs at Albany in 1989 were a career high, and he has shown some power in the majors, but he is more likely to pad his extra-base hit totals with doubles rather than home runs.

Age: 27			Bats: Right							Throws: Right		
	G	AB	H	2B	3B	HR	R	RBI	BB	SO	SB	BA
1990	92	303	78	13	1	5	28	25	27	51	2	.257
Career	Rookie year—career statistics same as above.											

KEVIN MAAS
FIRST BASE/OUTFIELD

Forget the inane home-run records he set in 1990. Does it really matter that he reached 15 career home runs faster than any other player in history? None of the players he passed for that record are in the Hall of Fame. More indicative of his immense potential is the praise he won from rival players. Oakland first baseman Mark McGwire—who possesses a Ph.D. in the science of longball—was particularly impressed. After watching one Maas moonshot, McGwire commented, "It's too bad this kid didn't come up until the middle of the season. If he had joined the Yankees right out of spring training, my rookie home-run record (49 in 1987) would be in jeopardy. He has a perfect Yankee Stadium swing." Despite the late start, Maas hit 21 homers in 1990. He is the first Yankee rookie to hit 20 or more home runs since Tom Tresh in 1962. His home-run total was also the third highest rookie mark in Yankee history. Only Joe DiMaggio and Joe Gordon hit more homers in their maiden seasons. (*Note:* It was erroneously reported in several newspapers that Bobby Murcer's 26 home runs in 1969 placed Maas fourth on the Yankee rookie list. However, under rules existing at that time, Murcer was not considered a rookie.) Maas should be more than a one-year wonder. After a steady breaking-ball diet put him into a late-season slump, he adjusted and was once again crushing the ball as the season closed.

Age: 26			Bats: Left							Throws: Left		
	G	AB	H	2B	3B	HR	R	RBI	BB	SO	SB	BA
1990	79	254	64	9	0	21	42	41	43	76	1	.252
Career	Rookie year—career statistic same as above.											

RANDY VELARDE

THIRD BASE/SHORTSTOP/LEFT FIELD

You would have to say Randy Velarde has a right to be angry. For a good part of the last four years he has been called the Yankee shortstop of the future, yet he was forced to sit as Wayne Tolleson, Rafael Santana, and now Alvaro Espinoza handled the position. Realizing he had little future at short, Velarde switched to third. He enjoyed a strong season at Columbus in 1989, hitting .266 with 40 extra-base hits in only 387 at-bats. Velarde also showed a natural proclivity for the hot corner. He has enough range for the position and a strong arm. The Yankees were impressed enough to recall him on July 28, 1989. The move was made following the ill-advised trade of Mike Pagliarulo to San Diego. Velarde was given Pags's third-base job. He hit .340 in 100 at-bats. This on top of a minor league season that saw him hit a career-high 11 home runs. You would think that would have clinched the spot for Velarde in 1990. However, he came to spring training and found that the third base job had all but been given to Mike Blowers. The result was a lost season, as Velarde watched Blowers, Wayne Tolleson, Jim Leyritz, and several others take their turns at third. Velarde was even put in left field, where the competition promised to be more heated than at third. If he is going to remain a Yankee, the team must find a way to utilize his talents. He doesn't seem to have the temperament to be a utility player, and he is too young and skilled to have to accept that role.

Age: 28			Bats: Right							Throws: Right		
	G	AB	H	2B	3B	HR	R	RBI	BB	SO	SB	BA
1990	95	229	48	6	2	5	21	19	20	53	0	.210
Career	184	466	106	16	4	12	52	43	35	97	1	.227

1990 SEASON

That which goes around . . . When George Steinbrenner bought the New York Yankees from the Columbia Broadcasting System in 1973, he took over a club with two established stars (Bobby Murcer and Thurman Munson), a consummate professional in the outfield (Roy White), a golden-gloved home-run hitter (Graig Nettles), a young left-handed slugger of seemingly limitless potential (Ron Blomberg), and a first-rate pitching staff headed by Mel Stottlemyre.

The last Yankee team to play under George Steinbrenner also featured two established stars (Don Mattingly and Steve Sax), a consummate professional in the outfield (Roberto Kelly), a golden-gloved home-run hitter (Jesse Barfield), and a young slugger of seemingly limitless potential (Kevin Maas)—but also an unrated pitching staff headed by no one. Although both teams finished below .500, there was at least one other major difference between them. The 1973 Yankees were a good team that didn't quite play up to its potential. In fact, they held first place for a lengthy period before the All-Star break. The 1990 Yankees, however, were your quintessential bad ball club. Very little went right for them during their forlorn season.

Baseball is a game meant to be played in the sun, but most of the Yankee summer was spent in the cold shadows cast by the Steinbrenner-Winfield mess. It commanded the media's attention throughout the season.

Steinbrenner had paid $40,000 to an admitted gambler who allegedly also worked for the charitable foundation run by Yankee outfielder Dave Winfield. The reason for the payment is a matter of dispute. At first, Steinbrenner claimed he gave the gambler the money as an inducement to change his life. Later, the Yankee owner claimed—in fact, he charged in criminal court—that the gambler had extorted the money by threatening to expose dark secrets involving Yankee employees.

The gambler had a different tale. He claimed he had sold to Steinbrenner information about fiscal abuses within the Winfield Foundation. This information was used by Steinbrenner in negotiations concerning annual contributions made by the Yankees to the Winfield Foundation. Steinbrenner had withheld these contributions pending an explanation of the alleged questionable practices and a change in the foundation's hierarchy. Though the particulars are still unknown, the subsequent negotiations between Steinbrenner and Winfield did result in a compromise that was generally viewed as favorable to the owner.

If you pierce the media murk that clung to this affair, a few facts become clear. George Steinbrenner was not called on the carpet by baseball commissioner Fay Vincent for buying information for use against a player. Instead, he was disciplined for his association with a known gambler. For that offense the commissioner was prepared to suspend Steinbrenner for two years. Why the owner chose a seemingly more stringent punishment—his removal as general partner—remains a mystery. The sentence allows Steinbrenner to continue in a limited role with the club. He can negotiate leases and television contracts, but he is prohibited from having any influence on baseball matters (i.e., trades, managerial moves, or free-agent signings). In order to attend Yankee games in the immediate future he must receive written permission from the commissioner's office.

Perhaps the Yankees' on-field struggles convinced "the Boss" it was time to end his reign. The Yankees have been a team in decline for five years. The 1990 club won four of its first five games, but the euphoria accompanying that start was short-lived. New York's starting pitching—wafer-thin as the team left spring training—was beset throughout the season by injury and inconsistency. Pascual Perez, having pitched brilliantly in his first three starts in April, suffered a shoulder injury and was sidelined for the season. Chuck Cary and Tim Leary would look unbeatable in one game and then quite ordinary in their very next mound appearance. Mike Witt pitched well after he was acquired from California in the Dave Winfield trade, but he also found himself on the disabled list for a lengthy period. (He did, however, return in September with several inspired performances.) Dave LaPoint did prove that his shoulder—injured in 1989—was again healthy. He pitched well but was victimized by inadequate support. Andy Hawkins's travails were symbolic of his team's season. He pitched a no-hitter against the Chicago White Sox—and lost. On the night that Chicago's Melido Perez (Pascual's younger brother) no-hit the Yankees, Hawkins was again the losing pitcher. If he had his best stuff and was able to limit his opponents to two or three runs, his teammates would forget how to score; on those days his teammates *did* remember how to hit, Hawkins would oftem get treated to an early shower by the opposition.

Of course, Hawkins wasn't the only Yankee pitcher to suffer from a paucity of runs. The Yankee offense sputtered for most of the season. Dave Winfield, trying to come back after missing all of 1989 with a back injury, couldn't find his timing. He was platooned, then benched, and eventually traded. Steve Sax, New York's offensive catalyst suffered through the worst season of his career. Alvaro Espinoza had a disastrous season at the plate, and Jesse Barfield remained inconsistent.

The final wound for the already hemorrhaging Yankee offense was inflicted when first baseman Don Mattingly was sidelined with a degenerative disc in July. Mattingly's back had troubled him all season. Even when he got off to the best April of his career, it was apparent that he wasn't attacking the ball with his customary brio. His power numbers were down and his early batting average was built on singles. As the season wore on, even the singles came less frequently. The loss of his 100-RBI bat and his fielding genius was crushing. On a positive note, however, Roberto Kelly showed continued improvement as a hitter, but even he was dogged by a mediocre first half.

Undermined by questionable starting pitching and a punchless offense, the Yankees stumbled to their worst season in almost 80 years. Bucky Dent, hired in 1989 to manage the team, was fired on June 6 and succeeded by Stump Merrill. Merrill's hiring signaled the onset of a Yankee youth movement. Kevin Maas, Oscar Azocar, and Jim Leyritz were brought up from the Columbus (triple-A) team to pump some life into the team's attack. Maas's left-handed power was especially welcome in Mattingly's absence, and he provided some late-season electricity for bereft Yankee fans. New York did manage to play its best ball after Merrill's hiring. The youngsters contributed on offense, and the starting pitching did improve. It was aided by the team's two strengths: a tight defense and the best bullpen in the division.

The Yankee youth movement continued in September with the call-up of Hensley Meulens, Dave Eiland, and Steve Adkins. Mattingly came back for several cameo appearances. His at-bats held the promise of a complete recovery for 1991. Off the field, former limited partner Robert Neiderlander was approved as Steinbrenner's successor by the American League owners in early September. He promised to leave the running of the club to his baseball people. These would include the Yankees' three-headed hierarchy: general manager Gene Michael, vice-president George Bradley, and manager Stump Merrill. This trio was handpicked by Steinbrenner before his departure, but they promised the Steinbrenner influence—one marked by rash judgments and reckless moves—had ended. In talking of the team's rebuilding program, all three men claimed to love challenges—they'd better.

George Steinbrenner

HISTORY

The most renowned franchise in sports started its American League life in 1901 as the Baltimore Orioles. League president Ban Johnson, wishing to compete with the National League on a head-to-head basis, moved the franchise to northern Manhattan in 1903. That team was known as the Highlanders, a name derived from its home field, Hilltop Park, which was situated on high land.

The New York squad was not an immediate success; it didn't win its first league championship until 1920. However, it did take part in a memorable pennant chase in 1904. Having dogged the front-running Boston Pilgrims through most of the season, the surprising Highlanders caught up with Boston in August and spent the rest of the summer in and out of first place. Highlander ace Jack Chesbro won his 41st game of the season (a modern major league record) on October 7, a 3-2 victory over the persistent Pilgrims. That win gave New York a half-game lead.

The euphoria that accompanied the dramatic win was short-lived. The day after the Chesbro victory, Boston swept a doubleheader to retake the lead. This set the stage for a final confrontation. An October 10th doubleheader between these two rivals would decide the league championship.

Chesbro, the Highlander ace, represented New York hopes in the first game. The 30-year-old right-hander was opposed by Boston's 22-game winner, Bill Dinneen. An inflamed crowd of 28,000 Highlander fans showed up to root their team to its first American League pennant. They would not go home happy. With the score tied 2-2 in the top of the ninth, Boston's Lou Criger found himself on third base with two men out. A Chesbro wild pitch sent Criger home with what proved to be Boston's pennant-clinching run.

The Highlanders would come close again in 1906, when a September swoon saw them land three games behind league-leading Cleveland. Chesbro, enjoying the last great season of his career, won 24 games for that team and was joined on the roster by future Hall of Famer Wee Willie Keeler.

The next 14 years were laced with mediocrity. New York took second place in 1910, but that team, now known as the Yankees, finished a disheartening 14½ games behind Connie Mack's muscular Philadelphia Athletics. The 1912 Yankees fielded one of baseball's all-time worst teams. It registered only 50 wins and finished 55 games behind first-place Boston. In 1913 the ragtag club left its home in Highland Park to share the Polo Grounds with the National League's New York Giants. The Yankees had become orphans.

Though few immediately recognized it, Yankee fortunes began to turn when the club was sold to Colonel Jake Ruppert and Tillinghast Huston in 1914. Both entrepreneurs were interested in owning more than just a baseball team. They wished to own a winning club. They backed this desire with their considerable fortunes and purchased such talents as pitchers Carl Mays and Bob Shawkey, catcher Muddy Ruel and third baseman Frank (Home Run) Baker. A third-place finish in 1919 was the first dividend on their investments.

Their spending spree reaped its greatest reward with the purchase of Babe Ruth from the Boston Red Sox on January 3, 1920. The reverberations from this single deal would ring strongly throughout all of baseball for the next several decades. It immediately altered the balance of power in the American League. Boston, which had been a contender for most of the prior 20 years, suffered a dramatic decline after the sale. The Ruth-led Yankees would soon be *the* power in baseball.

The Yankee success all stemmed from Ruth. He was the dominant player on baseball's dominant team. Having captured the public imagination with a record-setting 29 home runs in 1919, Ruth shattered that mark by hitting 54 homers in 1920. No other batter in either league would hit as many as 20. The performance elevated the Yankees to a third-place finish, only three games behind the world-champion Cleveland Indians.

An off-season trade with the Red Sox put right-hander Waite Hoyt and star catcher Wally Schang in Yankee uniforms for the 1921 season. They were the final stitches in the pennant fabric. With Ruth once again scything his own home-run record by hitting 59 balls out of the park, the Yankees won their first American League championship.

They would lose the World Series that year to the New York Giants. In 1922 the Yankees repeated as league champs, and once again fell to the Giants in October. Despite those two World Series wins, the Giants' front office grew increasingly wary of the Yankees' success. It informed its American League tenant that it was no longer welcome in the Polo Grounds.

This was a major faux pas. Forced to find new lodgings, Ruppert and Huston built Yankee Stadium, a dazzling 62,000-seat palace. Located less than a quarter of a mile from the Polo Grounds, it was the state-of-the-art ballpark of its time. The Yankees further nettled their now hated rivals by winning a third consecutive pennant in 1923 and by finally beating the Giants in the World Series, four games to one. The Yankees now stood on top of the baseball world. They had the finest stadium, the best team, and the greatest player in the game.

They briefly slipped from first place the next two seasons, but 1926 marked the beginning of the Yankee Era. That year a young first baseman named Lou Gehrig would join Ruth to form the most potent two-man offense in baseball history.

Babe Ruth

Photo: National Baseball Library, Cooperstown, N.Y.

They would form the heart of Murderers' Row and would help lead the team to four pennants and three world titles in the next seven years. The 1927 edition has been rightfully hailed as the greatest team ever. A testimony to its prowess can be found in that year's AL standings. The roster of the second-place Athletics contained the names of seven players who would eventually be enshrined in the Hall of Fame. Yet this talented club was fortunate to finish only 19 games behind the Yankees. Ruth once again led the team with a record-setting 60 home runs.

The Babe's career and Yankee fortunes started to decline in 1933. He left the club following the 1934 season, and his exit created a void that would eventually be filled in 1936 by a 21-year-old center fielder from San Francisco. Joe DiMaggio's fielding grace and incomparable batting skills would help lead the Yankees back to prominence for the next 16 years. During that time the Bronx Bombers would win 11 pennants and 10 world championships. Their success was unprecedented.

It continued into the 1950s and early 1960s. Casey Stengel, a former New York Giant, took over as manager of the club in 1949. The role of team superstar was passed from Joe DiMaggio to Mickey Mantle in 1951. The Yankees would win a record-setting five consecutive world championships from 1949 to 1953; 1955 to 1960 would bring five more pennants and two more world titles. The 1960 World Series loss to the Pittsburgh Pirates, on second baseman Bill Mazeroski's dramatic ninth-inning, final-game home run, closed out Stengel's tenure with the club. He was replaced as Yankee manager by Ralph Houk.

Houk's 1961 club rates just below the 1927 team as the greatest of all time. It certainly had the greatest home-run duo. Yankee right fielder and MVP Roger Maris broke the Babe's home-run record by hitting his 61st on the season's final day. He was chased throughout the summer by teammate Mantle, who settled for second place in the home-run derby with 54.

This was the last great Yankee team. New York would win three more consecutive pennants and one world championship, but its days of utter dominance had ceased. A depleted farm system, an early reluctance to sign black ball players, and unexpected injuries undermined the club. It finished sixth in 1965, the start of a decade-long era of darkness.

The team was acquired by CBS in 1964, then sold to shipbuilding magnate George Steinbrenner in 1972. He brought in general manager Gabe Paul to run the front office. Paul's shrewd maneuverings, coupled with the hiring of manager Billy Martin in 1975, brought the Yankees back to the fore. Steinbrenner further contributed by opening his wallet as wide as Ruppert and Huston had in their day. He enabled the Yankees to win the first big free-agent sweepstakes by signing Oakland's Cy Young Award winner Catfish Hunter to a five-year deal. Catfish contributed 17 wins as the Yankees won the pennant in 1976. Steinbrenner's generosity continued with the signings of slugger Reggie Jackson and ace left-hander Don Gullett. These 1977 additions helped New York win its first world championship in 15 years. The 1978 club, bolstered by the signing of reliever Goose Gossage and the remarkable performance of Cy Young Award winner Ron Guidry, repeated as world champions, but only after a dramatic midseason comeback and a playoff victory over the Boston Red Sox. That single-game playoff was turned around when Yankee shortstop Bucky Dent hit one of the most dramatic home runs in New York baseball history. It gave his team a lead it never relinquished.

New York won only two division titles and one pennant in the 1980s, but it was the winningest club of the decade. Individual honors went to 1985 MVP Don Mattingly and record-setting reliever Dave Righetti. The decade also saw the club graced by the steady excellence of right fielder Dave Winfield. After four consecutive noncontending seasons, the club embarked on a rebuilding program in 1990.

1990 TEAM LEADERS

BATTING

Roberto Kelly

Games .... Roberto Kelly	162
At-bats .... Roberto Kelly	641
Batting average .... Roberto Kelly	.285
Runs .... Roberto Kelly	85
Hits .... Roberto Kelly	183
Doubles .... Roberto Kelly	32
Triples .... Roberto Kelly	4
Home runs .... Jesse Barfield	25
On-base percentage ...... Jesse Barfield	.359
Slugging percentage ...... Roberto Kelly	.418
RBIs .... Jesse Barfield	78
Total bases .... Roberto Kelly	268
Walks .... Jesse Barfield	82
Most strikeouts .... Jesse Barfield	150
Stolen bases .... Steve Sax	43
Caught stealing .... Roberto Kelly	17

1990 TEAM LEADERS

PITCHING

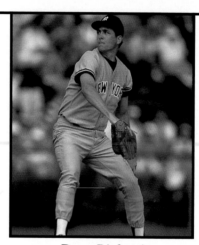

Dave Righetti

Games	Lee Guetterman	64
Wins	Lee Guetterman	11
Losses	Tim Leary	19
Starts	Tim Leary	31
Complete games	Tim Leary	5
Shutouts	Andy Hawkins, TimLeary, Mike Witt	1
Innings	Tim Leary	208
ERA	Tim Leary	4.11
Strikeouts	Tim Leary	138
Walks	Andy Hawkins	82
Saves	Dave Righetti	36
Relief appearances	Lee Guetterman	64
Winning percentage	Lee Guetterman	.611
Hits allowed	Tim Leary	202

1990 TRANSACTIONS

DATE	PLAYER	TRANSACTION
January 11	Tim Leary	Signed to one-year contract
January 23	Fred Toliver	Signed to one-year contract
January 24	Van Snider	Signed to one-year contract
January 30	Jimmy Jones	Signed to one-year contract
	Alan Mills	Signed to one-year contract
February 7	Eric Plunk	Signed to one-year contract, avoiding arbitration
February 8	Lance McCullers	Signed to one-year contract, avoiding arbitration
February 9	Lee Guetterman	Signed to one-year contract, avoiding arbitration
February 13	Randy Velarde	Signed to one-year contract
February 16	Willie Smith	Signed to one-year contract
February 21	Clay Parker	Signed to one-year contract
February 22	Dave Eiland	Signed to one-year contract
March 1	Brian Dorsett	Signed to one-year contract
March 2	Bob Geren	Signed to one-year contract
	Roberto Kelly	Signed to one-year contract
March 4	Alvaro Espinoza	Signed to one-year contract
	Greg Cadaret	Signed to one-year contract
March 6	Chuck Cary	Renewed contract
	Luis Polonia	Renewed contract
March 19	Deion Sanders	Signed to minor league contract
March 31	Britt Burns	Sent to minor league camp for reassignment
	John Fishel	Sent to minor league camp for reassignment
	Jim Leyritz	Sent to minor league camp for reassignment
	John Ramos	Sent to minor league camp for reassignment
	Dave Sax	Sent to minor league camp for reassignment
	Rob Sepanek	Sent to minor league camp for reassignment
April 1	John Habyan	Assigned to Columbus
April 2	Fred Toliver	Asked waivers for unconditional release
	Damasco Garcia	Asked waivers for unconditional release
	Willie Smith	Sent to minor league camp for reassignment
	Jim Walewander	Sent to minor league camp for reassignment
April 4	Dave Eiland	Optioned to Columbus
	Clay Parker	Optioned to Columbus
	Jeff Datz	Assigned to Columbus
	Jimmy Jones	Assigned to Columbus
April 5	Brian Dorsett	Optioned to Columbus
	Van Snider	Outrighted to Columbus
April 6	Lance McCullers	Placed on 15-day disabled list (bruised ribs)
	Clay Parker	Recalled from Columbus
April 9	Don Mattingly	Signed to five-year contract through 1995
April 15	Chuck Cary	Placed on 21-day disabled list (retroactive to April 9; inflamed left elbow)
April 16	John Habyan	Purchased from Columbus
April 24	Lance McCullers	Reinstated from the disabled list
	John Habyan	Outrighted to Columbus
April 29	Luis Polonia	Traded to California for Claudell Washington and Rich Monteleone
	Rich Monteleone	Reported to Columbus
April 30	Deion Sanders	Optioned to Columbus
	Pascual Perez	Placed on 15-day disabled list (retroactive to April 26; muscle strain in right shoulder)

DATE	PLAYER	TRANSACTION
May 11	Dave Winfield	Traded to California for Mike Witt
May 15	Chuck Cary	Reinstated from the disabled list
	Clay Parker	Optioned to Columbus
May 21	Deion Sanders	Recalled from Columbus
	Alan Mills	Optioned to Columbus
June 1	Pascual Perez	Transferred to 21-day disabled list
June 4	Lance McCullers	Traded to Detroit for Matt Nokes
	Clay Parker	Traded to Detroit for Matt Nokes
June 6	"Stump" Merrill	Named Yankee manager. Dismissed Bucky Dent
June 8	Rick Cerone	Placed on 21-day disabled list (damaged ligament in left knee)
	Mike Blowers	Optioned to Columbus
	Alan Mills	Recalled from Columbus
	Jim Leyritz	Purchased from Columbus
June 9	Mike Witt	Placed on 15-day disabled list (sore right elbow)
	Jimmy Jones	Purchased from Columbus
June 20	Claudell Washington	Placed on 15-day disabled list (retroactive to June 19; sprained right thumb)
	Mike Blowers	Recalled from Columbus
June 28	Deion Sanders	Optioned to Columbus
	Kevin Maas	Purchased from Columbus
July 12	Mike Blowers	Optioned to Columbus
	Deion Sanders	Recalled from Columbus
July 15	Mel Hall	Placed on 15-day disabled list (pulled right quadricep)
	Oscar Azocar	Purchased from Columbus
July 16	Mike Witt	Transferred to 21-day disabled list
	Pascual Perez	Transferred to 60-day disabled list
July 23	Lee Guetterman	Placed on 15-day disabled list (retroactive to July 19; muscle strain in right rib cage)
	Mark Leiter	Purchased from Columbus
July 27	Don Mattingly	Placed on 21-disabled list (lower back pains)
	Claudell Washington	Transferred to 30-day special disabled list
	Brian Dorsett	Recalled from Columbus
August 1	Deion Sanders	Placed on disqualified list
	Mel Hall	Reinstated from the disabled list
August 3	Lee Guetterman	Reinstated from the disabled list
	Alan Mills	Optioned to Columbus
August 6	Mark Leiter	Optioned to Columbus
	Mike Witt	Reinstated from the disabled list
August 9	Pascual Perez	Undergoes surgery on right shoulder
	Brian Dorsett	Optioned to Columbus
	Rick Cerone	Reinstated from the disabled list
August 19	"Stump" Merrill	Extended contract through 1992 season
September 9	Mike Blowers	Recalled from Columbus
	Brian Dorsett	Recalled from Columbus
	Dave Eiland	Recalled from Columbus
	Mark Leiter	Recalled from Columbus
	Alan Mills	Recalled from Columbus
	Steve Adkins	Purchased from Columbus
	John Habyan	Purchased from Columbus
	Hensley Meulens	Purchased from Columbus
	Jim Walewander	Purchased from Columbus
September 11	Don Mattingly	Reinstated from the disabled list
	Rich Monteleone	Purchased from Columbus
September 24	Deion Sanders	Asked waivers for unconditional release
October 4	Jimmy Jones	Outrighted to Columbus
	Jim Walewander	Outrighted to Columbus

DATE	PLAYER	TRANSACTION
October 5	Wayne Tolleson	Asked waivers for unconditional release
	Claudell Washington	Asked waivers for unconditional release
	Pat Kelly	Purchased from Albany
	Bernie Williams	Purchased from Albany
	Gerald Williams	Purchased from Albany
	Wade Taylor	Purchased from Columbus
October 22	Tim Leary	Declared free agency
	Dave Righetti	Declared free agency
	Jeff Robinson	Declared free agency

1991 ASSESSMENT

Before analyzing the future of this once-proud franchise, we have to first figure out who is running the show. Is George Steinbrenner truly out of the picture, or is he lurking in the Yankee Stadium catacombs like a mad Dr. Mabuse, trying to ignite the circuits of power with the electricity of his rage? A close observation of how the organization conducts its affairs may provide some hints.

The club's recent foray into the free-agent market does not render any clues. Robert Nederlander is the club's new general partner, and it was the Nederlanders who originally persuaded Steinbrenner that marquee names are a must in New York City — most of the shows they have backed on Broadway featured stars who supplied their own neon. More telling will be the treatment of management. If Stump Merrill and his coaches can survive the rough patches of sea, then perhaps the Steinbrenner influence is truly at an end. Keep an especially close eye on the pitching coach. In the past the Yankees have discarded pitching coaches as if they were Bic lighters.

Turning this team into an artistic success will require the patience that Yankee management has so often lacked. Kevin Maas could very well have a golden future, and Dave Eiland could help the starting rotation (as might Steve Adkins, if he can get his elusive knuckle-curve over home plate). But most of the other Yankees who came up from the minors last year are too old to be considered blue-chip prospects. The next wave — the one that will carry Bernie Williams, Darrin Chapin, Pat Kelly,

and Willie Smith — should be more fruitful.

It would not be a miracle if the Yankees were to contend in 1991. The AL East is the weakest division in baseball. However, a winning record this season is unlikely. The Yankees must first rebuild their once-powerful offense. The return of a healthy Don Mattingly and the continued progress of Kevin Maas, whom New York hopes to employ for a full season, will be a boon, but it won't be enough. Another left-handed bat is needed. Steve Sax has to rebound to his pre-1990 form (and it is a good bet that he will). His double-play partner, Alvaro Espinoza, has to hope that the return of Frank Howard will revive the sting in his bat. If it doesn't, this lineup cannot support his glove. A solid third baseman is a must.

Stump Merrill also must decide on the identity of his catcher. The Yankees' starting pitching has been a weakness for the last few years, and an unstable catching situation has not been the least of its problems. The club hasn't had a regular receiver since Butch Wynegar in 1985.

Of course, management's biggest priority will be to sort out a pitching staff. When was the last time the Yankees committed themselves to a starting rotation? It's been too long, and this club will not win or contend until it does. The return to health of Pascual Perez would be of immense help.

Clearly, there is too much to do in one season. However, the Yankees can be respectable while plotting the course for the team's return in '92.

PROSPECTS

HENSLEY MEULENS
Outfield

Hensley Meulens has had a roller-coaster minor league career. In 1987 he led the Carolina League in home runs with 28 while driving in 103 runs. A third baseman at the time, he also led the league in errors (37). However, he hit .300. Several major league clubs tried to acquire Meulens after that All-Star season. The Yankees chose to hold on to him. At first, it appeared to be a mistake. Meulens suffered through two mediocre seasons in 1988 and 1989. His power dropped off, and his fielding at third—never a strength—deteriorated even further. In 1990 the 23-year-old was switched to the outfield. More relaxed and confident, Meulens enjoyed his finest season yet, hitting .285 with 26 home runs and 96 RBIs for the triple-A Columbus Clippers. "Bam-Bam" still strikes out too often (132 times in 1990), but his right-handed power could put him in a Yankee uniform in 1991.

CARLOS RODRIGUEZ
Shortstop

A good-fielding shortstop in the Alvaro Espinoza mold, this 23-year-old has been held up by an unimpressive bat. His .252 at Albany in 1989 was a career high. However, Rodriguez made great strides at the plate in 1990, when he batted .273. Like Espinoza, he showed little power, but unlike the Yankee shortstop, he exhibited a surprising ability to get on base, drawing enough walks for a .360 on-base percentage. Rodriguez is an excellent contact hitter who rarely strikes out. As a switch-hitter with experience at second base, Rodriguez could join the Yankees as a valuable utility man. If Espinoza's hitting troubles continue, Rodriguez might even challenge him for the starting job.

STEVE ADKINS
Pitcher

The knock on Adkins has been his lack of an overpowering fastball, but he has been a winner throughout his minor league career. He got off to a slow start in 1990 but finished with a 15-7 record and a 2.90 ERA. Signed by the Yankees in 1986, the 25-year-old left-hander has developed a devastating "knuckle-curve" that has placed him among his league's strikeout leaders in each of the last two years. He has also developed a major league change-up. Yet Adkins has been plagued by control problems throughout his career, and the knuckle-curve, while often unhittable, has also proved to be erratic. If he can cut down on his walks, he could step into the Yankees' starting rotation sometime in 1991.

WILLIE SMITH
Relief Pitcher

At 6'6" and 240 pounds, Smith has a chance to be the most intimidating mound presence the Yankees have featured since the glory days of Goose Gossage. Smith is a reliever who came to the Yankees with Jeff Robinson in the deal that sent catcher Don Slaught to the Pittsburgh Pirates, and he is one of the hardest throwers in baseball—with the emphasis on "thrower." His speed terrorized opponents during the Yankees' 1990 spring training. Yet Smith needs to learn how to *pitch*. He must add another pitch to his repertoire and gain greater control over his other offerings. He walked nearly a man an inning at Columbus in 1990. However, when he did get the ball over the plate, opponents were often overmatched. Willie struck out 47 in only 34 innings. He will probably need at least another year of seasoning before he's ready for the major leagues.

MIKE BLOWERS
Third Base

Blowers won the Yankee's third base job during spring training, 1990, but then lost it shortly after the season began. Though noted as a fine fielder throughout his minor league career, he seemed tense and uncertain in the field with the Yankees. He made four errors in one game early in the season. He did get off to a decent start with the bat. He showed an ability to drive in runs, and his batting average against left-handers was outstanding. However, even that part of his game deteriorated, and he was soon back in the minor leagues. Blowers felt his hitting demise was partially the fault of bad coaching. In an interview after the season, the 25-year-old third baseman said, "[former Yankee batting coach Champ] Summers had some good ideas, things he wanted me to try, and they just didn't work for me personally." However, with the triple-A Columbus Clippers, Blowers came under the guidance of third base coach Clete Boyer, one of baseball's great enthusiasts and teachers. Inspired by Boyer's relentless encouragement, Blowers rediscovered his confidence. He now claims, "I basically got back to the way I was swinging the bat last year before I was traded [by Montreal to the Yankees]. Sending me down here and playing me was the best thing. It gave me a chance to find myself. I know I can play in the big leagues, and I know I'm going to." Blowers backed up these words by hitting .339 with 6 home runs and 50 RBIs in only 230 at-bats while with Columbus. He will get another chance in the major leagues during the 1991 season.

DAVE EILAND
Pitcher

It seems as if he has been a Yankee prospect forever, but this right-hander is only 24 years old. The Yankees had all but given up on him after two disappointing stints with the big-league club, but a 16-5 record, combined with a sparkling 2.87 ERA at Columbus, has revived their confidence. Like Adkins, Eiland does not have a big fastball. He does, however, have a varied repertoire assembled during three minor league seasons. It includes a good slider, a slow curve, a changeup, and a wicked sinker. Last year Eiland threw all four for strikes at any point in the count. If he can do that at the major league level, he will win a place in the Yankee rotation in 1991.

OTHER YANKEE PROSPECTS TO WATCH

Right-handed reliever Alan Mills has a great fastball but needs to develop his breaking ball and must refine his control. Seemed tentative during his stint with the Yankees. With experience and a good second pitch he could be a major league stopper.

Bernie Williams is a blue-chip prospect after hitting .338 in 1988, the center fielder saw his stock drop, along with his batting average, in 1989. Clearly, Williams had been rushed to triple-A too quickly. At double-A Albany in 1990, Williams resurrected his career by hitting .281 with 98 walks and 39 stolen bases. Improved patience at the plate was the key to his turnaround. Williams is an excellent fielder who combines speed and power. Only 22, he could join the Yankees in mid-1991. He is earmarked as the Yankee lead-off hitter of the future.

23-year-old second baseman Pat Kelly spent the summer at double-A Albany. A Steve Sax-type on offense, he has shown exceptional range and sure hands in the field. Kelly is also a gifted base runner who has stolen 80 bases in three minor league seasons. Two years away.

Mark Leiter is a 27-year-old left-hander, the brother of former Yankee Al Leiter. Shoulder problems have inhibited his career, but he seems healthy now. Leiter has a lively arm and has been used as a starter and reliever. He has an outside shot at making the Yankees in 1991.

Steve Adkins

Dave Eiland

KEY TRANSACTIONS

When the Yankees purchased Babe Ruth from the Boston Red Sox on January 3, 1920, it changed the balance of power, not just in the American League, but in all of baseball. The Red Sox, having won the World Series in 1915, 1916, and 1918, had been the AL's dominant club. A losing 1919 season and the financial setbacks suffered by club owner Harry Frazee forced the sale of Ruth to New York. The Yankees had been just another team throughout most of their history, but they had been gradually building a contender for several years. This deal put them over the top and started them on their long reign as baseball's most feared team. No transaction has ever made a greater impact on baseball history.

The purchase of Ruth also opened up a Boston-New York trading pipeline. Ruth was reunited with some of his Red Sox cronies on December 15, 1920, when the Yankees obtained Waite Hoyt, Wally Schang, Harry Harper, and Mike McNally from Boston for Muddy Ruel, Del Pratt, Sammy Vick, and Hank Thormahlen. Pratt was a 32-year-old star second baseman when the deal was consummated, and Ruel was an excellent young catcher. Pratt would have two outstanding years with losing Boston clubs, and Ruel two good seasons with those same teams before he was sent to Washington, where he played on pennant winners. Schang became the best catcher in the league, a fair trade-off for Ruel. But it was Hoyt who tipped this deal in favor of the Yankees. He turned out to be the Yankees' greatest right-hander ever and a future Hall of Famer.

On January 30, 1923, the Yankees received Herb Pennock from the Red Sox for Camp Skinner, Norm McMillan, George Murray, and $50,000. Toiling with poor Boston clubs, Pennock had just suffered two losing seasons. Once he was with the powerful Yankees, however, he proved he was one of the best left-handed pitchers in the major leagues. In his first year with the club he led the league in winning percentage (.760). He was a 21-game winner in 1924 and a 23-game winner in 1926, and he won 19 in two other years. Pennock teamed with Waite Hoyt to give the Yankees the best left-right pitching punch in baseball. Babe Ruth once named Pennock to his all-time All-Star team.

For the next 50 years, most of the deals between the Red Sox and Yankees were minor, though there was some talk of a deal involving Ted Williams and Joe DiMaggio. On March 22, 1972, however, the Yankees pulled off another heist. They obtained Sparky Lyle from Boston for Danny Cater and Mario Guerrero. This didn't seem like a bad deal at the time. Throughout his career Cater had hit like Rogers Hornsby in Fenway Park, and Guerrero was a promising minor league shortstop who had invited comparisons to Luis Aparicio. Lyle had been a good but erratic relief pitcher for the Red Sox. Once he got to Yankee Stadium, however, he became an All-Star. An immediate hit with the fans, Lyle saved a league-leading 35 games in 1972 and was one of the league's dominating relievers for the next five years. He won the Cy Young Award in 1977. Cater and Guerrero had little impact on

Boston, though Cater did have a fine year as a part-timer in 1973.

The man who eventually broke Babe Ruth's single-season home-run record did not come from Boston, but he did arrive in a trade. Roger Maris was obtained from the Kansas City Athletics for Hank Bauer, Don Larsen, Norm Siebern, and Marv Throneberry on December 11, 1959. Infielders Joe DeMaestri and Kent Hadley accompanied Maris on the trip. Maris was an instant success with the Yankees. He won the MVP Award in his first season in pinstripes and broke Ruth's record while earning another MVP in his second (1961). Maris drove in 100 or more runs in each of his first three Yankee seasons. He was a vital contributor to five successive New York pennants. During the last six weeks of the tight 1964 pennant race, Maris was probably the best player in baseball. More than just a slugger, the swift Maris was a punishing base runner and an outstanding outfielder with a powerful, accurate arm.

The Yankees fell from grace after 1964, but they rebuilt themselves into a power through a series of shrewd trades engineered by general manager Gabe Paul in the mid-1970s. One of them brought Lou Piniella from the Kansas City Royals for Lindy McDaniel on December 7, 1973. Why on earth would the Kansas City Royals trade a 30-year-old hustling outfielder with a lively bat for a 38-year-old reliever? The mystery endures. Although McDaniel had enjoyed an excellent 1973 season, the Kansas City bullpen wasn't particularly needy. The Royals even compounded matters by including pitcher Ken Wright in the deal—as if Piniella wasn't payment enough. Sweet Lou was that and more. Supplying the Yankees with a much-needed right-handed bat in a predominantly left-handed lineup, the fiery Piniella would star in New York for a decade. McDaniel pitched two seasons for the Royals, and then retired.

When Paul traded Bobby Bonds to California for Mickey Rivers and Ed Figueroa (December 11, 1975), a lot of observers thought he had slipped. Bonds represented the best package of speed and power in the business. Paul, however, knew that with the club returning to Yankee Stadium after a two-year exile in Shea Stadium, a swift center fielder was a must. He also judged that Bonds's right-handed bat would be somewhat muted by the Stadium's infamous Death Valley. Rivers had been the AL stolen-base champ in 1975. Though his arm was

Reggie Jackson

unimpressive, he could cover vast expanses of outfield territory, and his hitting and baserunning antics could make an offense go. Figueroa had won 16 games for the worst hitting team in baseball. It was an astute deal. Rivers would set the pace for three straight pennant-winning attacks, and Figueroa would win 55 games for those clubs, including 20 in 1978.

Paul also added speed, pitching, and defense with another trade that same day. He stole Willie Randolph, Dock Ellis, and Ken Brett from the Pittsburgh Pirates for George (Doc) Medich. Medich was an excellent pitcher who had won 49 games in three seasons for Yankee clubs that had had to scrape for runs. The Pirates assumed he would be a big winner with their "Lumber and Lightning" attack. Brett and Ellis had been injured in 1975, and Willie Randolph was an untested, although highly touted, minor leaguer. The trade was a boon for New York. Ellis won 17 games for the Bombers, and Brett (the older brother of Kansas City Royal superstar George Brett) was used as a trade-bait for White Sox outfielder Carlos May, a much-needed left-handed hitter for the Yankee bench. Willie Randolph made the transaction a steal. He was a Rookie of the Year candidate for the 1976 pennant-winning Yankees. A model of consistency, he cemented the club's infield for the next 13 years.

Ironically, Paul may have pulled off his best Yankee trade when he was still general manager of the Cleveland Indians. On November 27, 1972, he sent Graig Nettles and Gerry Moses to New York for John Ellis, Jerry Kenney, Charlie Spikes, and Rusty Torres. Ellis and Spikes had several good seasons for the Indians, and the trade was a good gamble for them. But it was a bonanza for the Yankees. The slick-fielding Nettles filled a hole at third that had been created by the exit of Clete Boyer in 1966. Nettles was a solid bat in his first three years as a Yankee, two of which were played in Shea Stadium (1974–75). With the team's return to Yankee Stadium in 1976, he exploded to win the AL home-run title (32). The following year he hit a career-high 37 home runs. Sparky Lyle believed that Nettles was MVP of the pennant-winning Yankees of 1976–78.

Whether or not that was true, the Yankees did not become world champions again until after the signing of Reggie Jackson on November 29, 1976. He was the most celebrated member of the first free agent class, and George Steinbrenner pulled out all the stops to sign him. Brash, charismatic, and always able to rise to the occasion, Jackson was the offensive time bomb the Yankees lineup needed to change it from merely excellent to great. Besides his power, Jackson brought an air of arrogant invincibility to the clubhouse. The 1976 Yankees had won a pennant but had lost the World Series in four straight to the Cincinnati Reds. Jackson, whose teams finished either in first or second place for 10 straight years (1969–1978), had played on three world champions as a member of the Oakland A's. As Willie Randolph later recalled, "He made us all a little bit better."

GREAT MOMENTS

When the Los Angeles Dodgers came to New York to face the Yankees in the opener of the 1977 World Series, they were a confident squad. Why not? Los Angeles could claim the National League's best attack. Four Dodgers—Steve Garvey, Ron Cey, Dusty Baker, and Reggie Smith—had combined for 125 home runs and 398 RBIs. Los Angeles second baseman Davey Lopes was one of the game's most accomplished base thieves. He had twice led the NL in stolen bases, and he possessed surprising power.

Los Angeles also had a quintet of reliable starters. Tommy John, a 20-game winner, led the staff and was the sort of left-hander who could give the Yankees fits. John had the best sinkerball in the majors. That pitch, delivered by a left-hander, was particularly effective in Yankee Stadium, especially against a New York lineup that was overloaded with left-handed power.

The rest of the rotation consisted of Don Sutton, Burt Hooton, Doug Rau, and Rick Rhoden. No other club could match this talented starting five. If these pitchers couldn't get the job done, then the game was placed in the hands of a bullpen whose only weakness was the lack of a reliable left-hander. This combination of speed, power, and pitching had proved insurmountable for National League rivals during the regular season. The Dodgers had won their division by 10 games over the powerful Cincinnati Reds. They had beaten an even stronger Philadelphia Phillie team in the National League playoffs. The team was primed for a World Series win.

But so were the Yankees, although they had not dominated their division as the Dodgers had theirs. This was not entirely New York's fault. The American League East was a stronger confederation than the National League West. Unlike the Dodgers, the Yankees had struggled to win their playoff series with the Kansas City Royals. Throughout the season, many doubted New York would even win their division. The team had been torn by dissension, most of it surrounding slugging right-fielder Reggie Jackson.

Jackson had been signed as a free agent during the winter of 1976. His was the most celebrated signing of that first free-agent wave. An integral part of the champion Oakland A's, Reggie was as outspoken as he was talented. When he joined New York, his proclamation that he was the "straw that stirred the drink" alienated many of his new teammates, especially MVP catcher Thurman Munson. He and others didn't like the way Jackson referred to himself in the third person, or how he would take out his wallet on the bus and start counting the $100 bills. This Yankee team had won an American League pennant in 1976; Jackson came to spring training acting as if he would be its savior. That was especially galling.

Yankee manager Billy Martin hadn't even wanted Jackson on the club. There was nothing personal in it. Martin's past contact with Jackson had been brief. He respected Jackson's hitting and baserunning abilities and his three World Series rings.

Martin simply felt that signing Reggie would not answer a crucial Yankee need. The club had plenty of left-handed power. Martin wanted a right-handed slugger to add balance to his lineup. His first choice in the free-agent draft would have been Oakland's Joe Rudi, a respected clutch hitter and the best left fielder in baseball. After Rudi he would have pursued Baltimore second baseman Bobby Grich (whom he would have played at shortstop) or Oakland designated hitter Don Baylor. Jackson would have been his fourth choice.

The Yankee front office gave no weight to Martin's suggestions. Rudi wasn't even drafted by New York. As a result, Jackson's signing was seen as an affront by the manager. Reggie's "magnitude of me" attitude and his other antics didn't endear him to his quick-tempered manager. The two were at odds almost from the first day of spring training.

The soap opera that evolved around Jackson hurt the team. More harmful were injuries to the pitching staff. Yankee ace Catfish Hunter was ineffective for most of the season. Ken Holtzman, a former 20-game winner, was suddenly unable to get anyone out. Left-hander Don Gullett, the Yankees' other big free-agent signee, was plagued by a sore arm throughout the first half of the season. These events conspired with the turmoil to keep the Yankees out of first place for most of the year. With each day that the club failed to live up to its own expectations, the pressure increased. Players started to air their gripes in the newspapers. It seemed as if the Yankees were going to self-destruct.

They didn't. They were much too talented for that. In mid-August the team came together. Differences were momentarily tossed aside as the team focused on winning a pennant and silencing its critics. The pitching staff, aided by the emergence of young Ron Guidry and the Cy Young Award–winning performance of reliever Sparky Lyle, muted enemy bats. The hitters butchered opposing pitchers. Martin, who had seemed distracted for a good part of the summer, managed brilliantly. As author Roger Angell later wrote: "Martin in the late weeks of this season was the best on-the-field manager I have ever seen. . . . his shifts of the batting order, his selections from a roster of often ailing or unsound pitchers, his late-inning picks of pinch-hitters or relief hurlers . . . must have left rival teams or managers at times with the feeling that they had not only been beaten up by the big-city slickers but somehow bamboozled as well."

Having survived so many on-field and off-field tests throughout the season, the Yankees were prepared for the Dodger challenge. The first Series game was filled with enough tension for an Indiana Jones movie. Los Angeles grabbed a quick two-run lead off Gullett in the first inning. New York answered with an immediate run in their half of the frame, tied the game at 2-2 in the sixth, and took a one-run lead in the eighth. The Dodgers came back with a run in the top of the ninth. With the game now in jeopardy, Martin called on Sparky Lyle. The left-hander shut out the Dodgers for four innings. He was the winning pitcher when Yankee second baseman Willie Randolph was driven home by back-up center fielder Paul Blair in the 12th. Blair had gotten an essential hit in the crucial fifth game of the American League playoffs. His performance was a testament to the depth of the Yankee bench.

Los Angeles returned the next day with a 6-1 drubbing of the home team. Catfish Hunter's ailing arm couldn't keep the Dodgers in check. Los Angeles mugged the future Hall of Famer for four home runs. Catfish didn't make it past the third inning.

The scene switched to Los Angeles, and the Dodgers were convinced they had an immediate edge. The next three games would be in their home park, where they had been nearly unbeatable all season. The starting pitcher for Game 3 would be their ace, Tommy John, who had been especially tough against the Yankees throughout his American League career.

Mike Torrez, a 17-game winner, started for New York. The Yankees took a three-run lead in the first. Los Angeles tied it in the third, but Yankee runs in the fourth and fifth sealed a 5-3 victory. The loss was especially injurious to the Dodger cause. The team's best pitcher had failed. John had pitched the final game of National League playoffs. That had prevented him from appearing in the Series until the third game. Unless the Series went the full seven, the Dodger ace would be unable to start again.

Ron Guidry put the Dodgers in an even more precarious position in Game 4. The young left-hander had been knocked out early by the Royals in the final game of the playoffs. His control had been off, and his slider, his main weapon of choice, had been erratic. On this day against the Dodgers, however, the slider was nearly unhittable. The Dodgers scored two runs, on only four hits, while losing to New York 4-2. Los Angeles was down three games to one and was on the verge of elimination.

Don Sutton arrived with a stay of execution for Game 5. The right-hander wasn't quite as sharp as he had been in his Game 1 loss to New York—this time he surrendered four runs on nine hits.

However, by the time the first of those Yankee runs had scored, Los Angeles had already built a 10-run lead.

The Dodgers now had reason for hope. Mike Torrez was slated to start for the Yankees in Game 6. He had beaten the Dodgers in Game 3, but Los Angeles had been able to reach him for three runs, and Torrez had to be a tired pitcher. In the playoffs he had pitched five innings of relief against the Royals only two days after he had pitched nearly six innings as a starter. He had also thrown a lot of pitches in his victory over the Dodgers.

Hooton, on the other hand had not been overly taxed either during the regular season or by post-season play. He had pitched brilliantly against the Yankees in his Game 2 victory. Another similar performance, and the Series would come down to a seventh game. John would start that contest, and no one on the Dodgers believed the Yankees would be able to beat the southpaw a second time.

Los Angeles scored two runs in the first; New York tied it with two in the second. A run in the third gave Los Angeles a 3-2 advantage. With Thurman Munson on base, Reggie Jackson stepped to the plate in the fourth. Jackson had already homered twice in the Series. Though no one realized it at the time, he was about to stamp his imprimatur on the game, the Series, and the season. When Burt Hooton delivered his first pitch, a fastball near the heart of the plate, Jackson attacked it as if he were a hungry child leaping for dessert. He sent the ball deep into the right-field stands for a lead the Yankees would never relinquish.

One inning later, Reggie came up with two out and Willie Randolph on first. Reliever Elias Sosa had succeeded Hooton to the mound, but he had no more success with Reggie than the fallen starter had. Sosa's first pitch was a fastball that Reggie transformed into a searing line drive, a heat-seeking missile that never stopped until it forced its way into the third row of the right-field seats. It was not as majestic a home run as the first, but it was perhaps more impressive for its display of sheer power. Had that angry line drive hit the Stadium wall, it probably would have put a hole in it.

When Reggie came up in the eighth, the Yankees had a 7-3 lead. There would be no fastballs for this outing. Dodger reliever Charlie Hough was on the mound, and he was the master of the knuckleball. Hough started Jackson off by uncorking a beauty of a knuckler, a drunken butterfly that careened up to the plate low and away. A pitcher's pitch. It didn't matter. Reggie sent it into the center-field seats. The Dodgers were done. The blasts put Reggie in the record books and helped New York to its first world

championship in 13 years. Reggie also did something more. He gave baseball fans everywhere something to store in the warehouse of their most cherished baseball memories. Three pitches, three swings, three home runs—rockets that illuminated a clear, dark October night in the Bronx.

Reggie! Reggie! Reggie!: Reggie Jackson's three home runs crush the Dodgers in the final game of the 1977 World Series (October 18, 1977)

ALL TIME ALL STAR TEAM

FIRST BASE ★ LOU GEHRIG

The Iron Horse played in 2,130 consecutive games and made an offensive impact in almost every one of them. An able, if unacrobatic, first baseman, Gehrig was noted for his breath-taking hitting accomplishments. He led the American League in RBIs five times, including a league-record 184 in 1931. From 1927 to 1937 he *averaged* 153 runs batted in. Gehrig played 14 full seasons; he drove in at least 100 runs in all but one of them. His RBIs-per-games-played ratio is the best in baseball history. Though Gehrig was a left-handed hitter, he was not particularly helped by Yankee Stadium's right-field porch. During the 1930 season, the first baseman hit 27 home runs and had 117 RBIs—on the road! He wreaked all that havoc in only 78 games.

SECOND BASE ★ TONY LAZZERI

Tony Lazzeri was a right-handed power hitter whose best shots were absorbed by Yankee Stadium's dreaded Death Valley. Despite this, he was one of his era's most feared sluggers and clutch hitters. Poosh 'Em Up Tony was always expected to deliver with men on base, and more often than not he did. He drove in 100 or more runs seven times and finished third in the league in home runs twice. Lazzeri had an excellent batting eye and was a gifted baserunner. He stole 22 bases in 1927 without getting thrown out. At second base, only Detroit's Charlie Gehringer was rated above him defensively, and Lazzeri was equally adept at short. The 1932 World Series provided his finest moments as a Yankee. In New York's four-game sweep of the Cubs, Lazzeri hit two home runs and had five RBIs.

SHORTSTOP ★ PHIL RIZZUTO

When Ted Williams was asked why his Boston powerhouses continually lost pennants to the Yankees, he often replied, "Because of that little guy at shortstop. He was the difference between our two teams." For the better part of his career, Rizzuto was the best fielding shortstop in the American League. Hitting at the top of the strong Yankee lineup, he was expected to get on base and score ahead of his slugging teammates. Rizzuto fulfilled this with stinging line drives, walks, and the deadliest bunting style in baseball. In 1949 many thought his overall play was worthy of the MVP Award. He didn't win. He made up for it the following season by taking the prize. Rizzuto spent 13 years as the Yankees' starting shortstop. They finished first in nine of those seasons.

THIRD BASE ★ GRAIG NETTLES

Throughout their championship years, the Yankees were usually blessed with superior third basemen. Frank Baker, Jumpin' Joe Dugan, and Red Rolfe all brought prestige to the position. None of them could equal the fielding genius of Clete Boyer, the acrobatic magician who played on five straight Yankee pennant winners in the early to mid-1960s. Yet not even Boyer could combine fielding dexterity with offensive power the way Graig Nettles did. A left-handed slugger, Nettles was born to hit in Yankee Stadium. Though his lifetime batting average was only .248, he made up for it with 390 career home runs and an on-base percentage of .332. Nettles won a home-run crown in 1976. His dazzling heroics in Game 3 of the 1978 World Series turned matters around for the Yankees. He was the best fielding third baseman of the 1970s.

LEFT FIELD ★ MICKEY MANTLE

Mantle was baseball's most formidable offensive force for over a decade. Not one of his peers, not even the nonpareil Willie Mays, possessed his combination of animal speed and savage power. As an outfielder, he wasn't nearly the equal of Mays or DiMaggio. He lacked their defensive instincts. But he compensated with sheer talent and his unfathomable speed. Though the Yankee offense rarely showcased the stolen base, Mantle could steal bases practically at will. He was successful in over 80 percent of his attempts. After retiring, Mantle expressed regret at finishing with a batting average below .300 (.298). However, his lifetime on-base percentage (.423) is 13th on the all-time list. He is the career leader in World Series home runs (18).

CENTER FIELD ★ JOE DIMAGGIO

More than just an amalgam of intelligence, talent, and daring, DiMaggio was a presence. He could inspire teammates to envision victory by simply striding into the clubhouse. He epitomized grace as a fielder. DiMaggio could cover vast expanses of real estate with effortless strides. He was an even better hitter. Yankee Stadium is doom for right-handed sluggers, yet DiMaggio won two home-run titles, two RBI crowns, and two batting championships. His 56-consecutive-game hitting streak may not be unassailable, but it has withstood batters' assaults for 50 years. DiMaggio hit 361 career home runs while striking out only 369 times. He played 13 seasons. He was an All Star in each of them and played in 10 World Series. Few careers have enjoyed such unrelenting success.

RIGHT FIELD ★ BABE RUTH

Simply the greatest ballplayer to ever grace a diamond. Ruth was baseball. His star rose in the 1920s, a period that celebrated excess. If the era hadn't produced Ruth as its hero, F. Scott Fitzgerald would have had to create him. Half-measures were unknown to Ruth. He lived big, ate big, and swung big. No contemporary could hit as many home runs or hit them farther. Ruth out-homered entire teams. He won 12 home-run titles and led the league in RBIs six times and in runs scored, eight times. His career on-base percentage is baseball's second highest. His lifetime slugging percentage—a staggering .690—is unsurpassed. The Babe was also an excellent outfielder. Former teammates and opponents claim he rarely made a mistake on the playing field.

CATCHER ★ YOGI BERRA

Yogi Berra was the MVP of the 1950s. Not a particularly skilled catcher when he first came up, Berra worked zealously with Hall of Fame receiver Bill Dickey and pitchers Allie Reynolds and Vic Raschi until he became a defensive plus. Yogi holds the record for most consecutive games and chances without an error. His hitting ability was never a question. He amassed 358 home runs and a lifetime .285 batting average. A clutch performer, he was called the most dangerous hitter in baseball after the seventh inning. Berra was a three-time MVP (1951, '54, '55) and finished in the top four in every MVP balloting from 1950 to 1956. He received at least two MVP votes every year from 1947 to 1961.

LEFT-HANDED STARTER ★ WHITEY FORD

Ford's .690 lifetime winning percentage is the best of any 200-game winner in baseball history. Ford led the American league in victories three times and in ERA twice. His 25-4 record in 1961 netted him the Cy Young Award as baseball's best pitcher. The Chairman of the Board was best known as a tough man in the clutch. Ford was at his best in World Series competition. He holds World Series records for wins (10), strikeouts (94), and innings pitched (146). Pitching against National League champions, he compiled a sparkling 2.71 ERA.

RIGHT-HANDED STARTER ★ WAITE HOYT

Schoolboy was 18 when he pitched his first major league game for John McGraw's New York Giants in 1918. He was sent to Boston and the AL in 1919. Still learning his trade, he had two mediocre seasons with that club but pitched well enough to impress Yankee general manager Ed Barrow. Hoyt came to the Yankees as part of an eight-player deal after the 1920 season. He was an immediate success with the Yankees. From 1921 to 1928, he notched 145 wins, including a league-leading 22 in 1927. In six World Series with New York he was 6-3 with a 1.83 ERA. A modest man, he once claimed the secret to winning was "pitching for the Yankees."

RELIEF PITCHER ★ GOOSE GOSSAGE

From 1978 to 1982 Gossage was the dominant mound force in the American League. Kansas City outfielder Clint Hurdle called him the "Master of Disaster." On a team of superstars, Gossage was the most feared Yankee. During that five-year stretch, he saved 128 games and compiled a 2.10 ERA. The Goose often got off to slow starts, but as the weather warmed, his fastball would blaze. As he strode in from the bullpen, opponents knew they had little chance to pick up the chips on the table; Gossage was going to close the deal.

RECORD HOLDERS

CAREER

BATTING

Games	Mickey Mantle	2,401
At-bats	Mickey Mantle	8,102
Batting average	Babe Ruth	.349
Runs	Babe Ruth	1,959
Hits	Lou Gehrig	2,721
Doubles	Lou Gehrig	535
Triples	Lou Gehrig	162
Home runs	Babe Ruth	659
Grand slams	Lou Gehrig	23
Total bases	Lou Gehrig	5,060
Slugging percentage	Babe Ruth	.710
RBIs	Lou Gehrig	1,991
Extra-base hits	Lou Gehrig	1,190
Bases on balls	Babe Ruth	1,847
Strikeouts	Mickey Mantle	1,710
Stolen bases	Rickey Henderson	326

PITCHING

Games	Dave Righetti	522
Wins	Whitey Ford	236
Losses	Mel Stottlemyre	139
Starts	Whitey Ford	438
Complete games	Red Ruffing	261
Shutouts	Whitey Ford	45
Innings	Whitey Ford	3,171
ERA	Russell Ford	2.54
Strikeouts	Whitey Ford	1,956
Walks	Lefty Gomez	1,090
Saves	Dave Righetti	224
Relief appearances	Dave Righetti	446
Winning percentage	Spud Chandler	.717

Rickey Henderson

Ron Guidry

RECORD HOLDERS

SEASON

BATTING

Games	Bobby Richardson (1961), Roy White (1970), Chris Chambliss (1978), Don Mattingley (1986), Roberto Kelly (1990)	162
At-bats	Bobby Richardson (1962)	692
Batting average	Babe Ruth (1923)	.393
Runs	Babe Ruth (1921)	177
Hits	Don Mattingly (1986)	238
Doubles	Don Mattingly (1986)	53
Triples	Earle Combs (1927)	23
Home runs	Roger Maris (1961)	61
Grand slams	Don Mattingly (1987)	6
Total bases	Babe Ruth (1921)	457
Slugging percentage	Babe Ruth (1920)	.847
RBIs	Lou Gehrig (1931)	184
Extra-base hits	Babe Ruth (1921)	119
Bases on balls	Babe Ruth (1923)	170
Most strikeouts	Jesse Barfield (1990)	150
Fewest strikeouts	Joe Sewell (1932)	3
Stolen bases	Rickey Henderson (1988)	93

PITCHING

Games	Dave Righetti (1985, 1986)	74
Wins	Jack Chesbro (1904)	41
Losses	Joe Lake (1908)	22
Starts	'Jack Chesbro (1904)	51
Complete games	Jack Chesbro (1904)	48
Shutouts	Ron Guidry (1978)	9
Innings	Jack Chesbro (1904)	455
ERA	Spud Chandler (1943)	1.64
Strikeouts	Ron Guidry (1978)	248
Walks	Tommy Byrne (1949)	179
Saves	Dave Righetti (1986)	46
Relief appearances	Dave Righetti (1985, 1986)	74
Winning percentage	Ron Guidry (1978)	.893

TRIVIA QUIZ

1. What left-handed pitcher for the Red Sox nearly no-hit the Yankees on April 14, 1967? He lost his no-hit bid when Yankee catcher Elston Howard singled with two out in the ninth inning.

2. What right-hander was the winning pitcher when Chris Chambliss hit his dramatic ninth-inning home run to win the deciding game of the 1976 American League playoffs?

3. Who was the Yankee scout who signed both Mickey Mantle and Bobby Murcer?

4. What pitcher surrendered the first hit in Joe DiMaggio's 56-game hitting streak in 1941?

5. The roster of the 1979 Yankees included 10 men who at one time or another won a Gold Glove Award. Name them.

6. Who was the first Yankee to lead the league in home runs?

7. Who was the first Yankee to lead the league in stolen bases?

8. Who was at bat when Babe Ruth was thrown out attempting to steal second for the final out of the 1926 World Series?

9. Who was the first Yankee to bat in a regular-season game in Yankee Stadium?

10. Who was the only pitcher on the 1927 Yankees to suffer a losing record?

ANSWERS ON PAGE 63

1991 SCHEDULE

APRIL

SUN	MON	TUE	WED	THU	FRI	SAT
	1	2	3	4	5	6
7	8 DET 1:35	9	10 DET 1:35	11 DET 1:35	12 KC 8:35	13 KC 2:35
14 KC 2:35	15 CHI 1:00	16 CHI 7:30	17 CHI 1:00	18	19 KC 7:30	20 KC 1:30
21 KC 1:30	22 DET 7:30	23 DET 7:30	24 DET 7:30	25	26 CHI 8:05	27 CHI 7:05
28 CHI 2:35	29	30 OAK 10:05				

MAY

SUN	MON	TUE	WED	THU	FRI	SAT
			1 OAK 3:15	2	3 SEA 10:35	4 SEA 10:05
5 SEA 4:35	6 SEA 10:05	7 CAL 10:35	8 CAL 10:35	9	10 OAK 7:30	11 OAK 1:30
12 OAK 1:30	13 OAK 7:30	14 CAL 7:30	15 CAL 7:30	16 CAL 7:30	17 SEA 7:30	18 SEA 1:30
19 SEA 1:30	20 CLE 7:35	21 CLE 7:35	22 CLE 7:35	23	24 BAL 7:35	25 BAL 7:35
26 BAL 1:35	27 BOS 1:00	28 BOS 7:30	29 BOS 7:30	30	31 MIL 7:30	

JUNE

SUN	MON	TUE	WED	THU	FRI	SAT
						1 MIL 1:30
2 MIL 1:30	3 TOR 7:30	4 TOR 7:30	5 TOR 7:30	6	7 TEX 7:30	8 TEX 7:30
9 TEX 1:30	10	11 MIN 8:05	12 MIN 8:35	13 MIN 8:05	14 TEX 8:35	15 TEX 8:35
16 TEX 8:35	17	18 TOR 7:35	19 TOR 7:35	20 TOR 7:35	21 MIN 7:30	22 MIN 7:30
23 MIN 1:30	24 MIN 7:30	25 BOS 7:35	26 BOS 7:35	27 BOS 7:35	28 MIL 8:35	29 MIL 8:35
30 MIL 2:35						

☐ Home games   ☐ Road games

OT — Oldtimers Day   • 60 •

JULY

SUN	MON	TUE	WED	THU	FRI	SAT
	1 CLE 7:30	2 CLE 7:30	3 CLE 7:30	4 BAL 1:00	5 BAL 7:30	6 BAL 1:30
7 BAL 1:30	8	9 ALL-STAR GAME	10	11 CAL 10:35	12 CAL 10:35	13 CAL 10:05
14 CAL 4:05	15 SEA 10:05	16 SEA 3:35	17	18 OAK 10:05	19 OAK 10:35	20 OAK 4:05
21 OAK 4:05	22	23 SEA 7:30	24 SEA 7:30	25 SEA 1:00	26 CAL 7:30	27 OT CAL 2:00
28 CAL 1:30	29 OAK 7:30	30 OAK 7:30	31 MIN 7:30			

AUGUST

SUN	MON	TUE	WED	THU	FRI	SAT
				1 MIN 1:00	2 DET 7:35	3 DET 7:35
4 DET 1:35	5 DET 7:35	6 CHI 8:05	7 CHI 8:05	8 CHI 3:05	9 DET 7:30	10 DET 7:30
11 DET 1:30	12	13 KC 7:30	14 KC 7:30	15 KC 1:00	16 CHI 7:30	17 CHI 7:30
18 CHI 1:30	19 KC 8:35	20 KC 8:35	21 KC 8:35	22	23 TOR 7:35	24 TOR 1:35
25 TOR 1:35	26 TEX 7:30	27 TEX 7:30	28 TEX 7:30	29 TOR 7:30	30 TOR 7:30	31 TOR 1:30

SEPTEMBER

SUN	MON	TUE	WED	THU	FRI	SAT
1 TOR 1:30	2 TEX 3:05	3 TEX 8:35	4 TEX 8:35	5	6 MIN 8:05	7 MIN 8:05
8 MIN 2:05	9 BAL 7:35	10 BAL 7:35	11 BAL 7:35	12 BOS 7:30	13 BOS 7:30	14 BOS 1:30
15 BOS 1:30	16 MIL 7:30	17 MIL 7:30	18 MIL 7:30	19	20 BOS 7:35	21 BOS 1:05
22 BOS 1:05	23 MIL 8:35	24 MIL 8:35	25 MIL 8:35	26 MIL 8:35	27 CLE 7:35	28 CLE 1:35
29 CLE 1:35	30 CLE 7:35					

OCTOBER

SUN	MON	TUE	WED	THU	FRI	SAT
		1 BAL 7:30	2 BAL 7:30	3 BAL 7:30	4 CLE 7:30	5 CLE 1:30
6 CLE 1:30	7	8	9	10	11	12

COLLECTOR'S CORNER

NOTES
&
AUTOGRAPHS

Ain't no fences high enough.

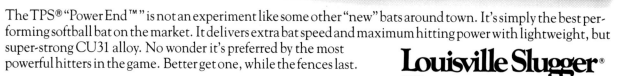

The TPS® "Power End™" is not an experiment like some other "new" bats around town. It's simply the best performing softball bat on the market. It delivers extra bat speed and maximum hitting power with lightweight, but super-strong CU31 alloy. No wonder it's preferred by the most powerful hitters in the game. Better get one, while the fences last.

Louisville Slugger®

Hillerich & Bradsby Co. Louisville, Kentucky
Say yes to sports, say no to drugs!